# Spring
# Peepers
# Are
# Calling

# Spring Peepers Are Calling

**Charlene W. Billings**

Illustrated by Susan Bonners

DODD, MEAD & COMPANY · NEW YORK

ACKNOWLEDGMENTS

I gratefully acknowledge the guidance and many helpful sugges-
tions given me by my editor, Rosanne Lauer, and by my husband,
Barry.

Library of Congress Cataloging in Publication Data

Billings, Charlene W
    Spring peepers are calling.

    SUMMARY: Discusses the life cycle of the spring
peeper and the capture and care of this tiny tree
frog as a pet.
    1.  Hyla crucifer—Juvenile literature.
[1.  Tree frogs.  2.  Frogs as pets.  3.  Pets]
·I.  Bonners, Susan.  II.  Title.
QL668.E24B54        597'.8        78-7735
ISBN 0-396-07584-3

*For Cheryl and Sharon*

A late afternoon spring breeze passes over the open pond. The ice melted away several weeks ago.

All along the edge of the pond, plants are beginning to turn green again, as they have for countless springs. The pussy willows already have developed green seedpods, the woodland violets are just starting to bloom, and the skunk cabbages are unfurling their leaves to the sun.

In among the grasses at the pond's edge, animals are beginning activity again after the long winter.

As dusk arrives, a sound floats over the air.

*Pee-EEp! Pee-EEp!*

*Pee-EEp! Pee-EEp!*

At the start, there is only one voice. The lower first tone of the high-pitched *pee-EEp* seems to slide into the second higher tone.

7

Within moments there are a few voices.

Then there is a loud unending chorus of *pee-EEp*, *pee-EEp*, *pee-EEp* penetrating the spring night. The peeping can be heard half a mile away, or more. At that distance, it sounds almost like sleigh bells.

Amazingly, the source of all this peeping is the tiny tree frog called the spring peeper.

Many people call spring peepers by other common names such as peepers, peeping frogs, Pickering's tree frogs, or castanet tree frogs. On Martha's Vineyard, they are called "pinkletinks." The scientific name for spring peepers is *Hyla crucifer*. This does not change from place to place.

The first part of the scientific name, *Hyla*, means tree frog. The second part of the scientific name, *crucifer*, means cross-bearing. This name was chosen because of a brown X which appears on the back of the spring peeper. On some individuals, the X may not be perfect and may look more like an inverted Y, but the mark does resemble a cross, and so the name *crucifer*.

Spring peepers usually have brown or gray-green skin,

with bands of darker color on their back legs. Their bellies are pale yellow. On warm summer days, their skin often changes to a lighter color; this helps them feel cooler. Even you probably change from dark-colored clothing to light-colored clothing in summer for the same reason.

Spring peepers differ from true frogs in that they have a small pad on the end of each toe. There is a sticky adhesive on the undersurface of these pads from glands within the toes. With these special pads, spring peepers can cling to almost any surface, even if it is slippery.

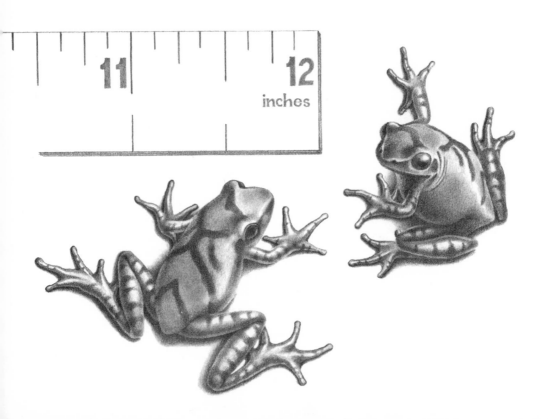

Both males and females hear sounds with eardrums located just behind and a little below their eyes.

Only the male spring peepers sing. The females are silent. The males are about one inch long, surprisingly small to have such loud voices. While they sing, the peepers are often found clinging to a few blades of grass or a twig at the water's edge.

The male peeper has a special vocal sac located on his throat, just below his mouth. It is a single pocketlike

pouch of loosely hanging skin that bubbles out when he pumps air into it. In fact, when the vocal sac is filled with air, it looks like a bubble almost as big as he is. The male peeps by closing his mouth and nostrils and pumping air back and forth over his vocal cords between his lungs and vocal sac. The sac itself greatly magnifies the sound.

Each male peeper is trying to attract a female with his peeping. Without his voice, males and females would have difficulty finding each other to reproduce.

The peeping continues as dusk disappears into darkness.

If a male senses the presence of a female spring peeper nearby, at the edge of the pond, he stops his peeping and hops over to her. The female is usually slightly larger than the male, about one and one-quarter inches long. She is attracted by the spring sound of the male peeper.

Because it is dark now, the male and female must recognize each other by voice and touch.

The female spring peeper carries hundreds of unlaid eggs inside her body. But her eggs will not develop unless they are fertilized by sperm from a male.

The male follows the female into shallow water. He positions himself on her back and tightly hugs her just behind her forearms. As she lays her eggs, one by one, he releases a pale liquid containing sperm onto each of them. The peepers move together from spot to spot until all of the eggs are laid. Now she returns to the woods until next spring. The male may remain at the pond and continue to call for a few more weeks before he too returns to the woods.

Each fertilized egg is surrounded by a sticky jelly and clings singly to the underwater stem of a plant. Some of

the eggs may stray to the bottom, where they drift loosely. Each egg is very tiny, measuring only about 1/12 of an inch. At first, the egg is deep brown above and white below. As it develops, the egg becomes light gray. Most of the eggs will hatch in about five to fifteen days, depending upon the temperature of the water. However, some of the eggs will be eaten by leeches, small fish, larvae of water beetles, dragonfly nymphs, and even peeper tadpoles that hatched a few days earlier.

Each surviving spring peeper egg hatches into a small, hungry tadpole.

These tadpoles have sharp little *rasps* or teeth on their
lips with which they scrape small, green plants called
*algae* from the surfaces of rocks and other larger plants
in the pond for food. They find plenty of algae to eat.
Algae may even cover some areas of the pond surface
like a green scum. The algae are a living, growing part of
the pond.

Tadpoles look more like fish than frogs. Each has a
tail that is waved or wiggled from side to side to swim
through the water. Like a fish, a tadpole breathes with
gills instead of lungs. It takes water into its mouth and

passes it over its gills where the oxygen in the water is absorbed. Then the water passes out through a single small opening on the tadpole's left side called a *spiracle*.

At this stage of life, the tadpoles have no legs at all.

Spring peeper tadpoles appear iridescent. Their colors are shiny and seem to alter with changes in the light. Their backs are orange, with big dark spots and small gold spots. Gold and silver marks decorate the area in front of their gills. Underneath, they are a reddish-bronze color. They are tadpoles for about ninety to one hundred days —that is, if they aren't eaten first!

Fortunately, there are some safe hiding places found among the grasses and other plants in the water. If some of the tadpoles swim out from these grasses in the shallow area of the pond, they may be swallowed by a small fish

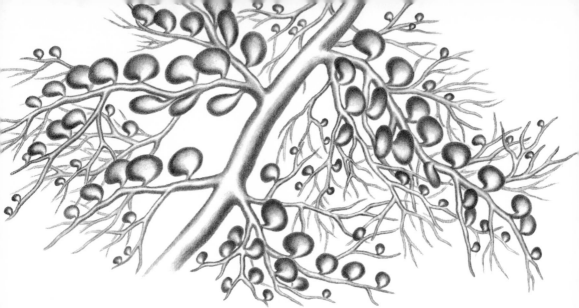

or some other enemy. There are giant water bugs, larger fish, turtles, newts, and even big frogs in the water that eat tadpoles. Larger tadpoles eat smaller tadpoles, even of their own species.

As if all of the animal enemies aren't enough, there are even plant enemies. A plant called *bladderwort* has tiny sacs on the edges of its fine leaves. Each sac has a small door. The entire sac and the door are squeezed shut. When an unsuspecting tadpole, or other small water animal, touches the sensitive hairs at the edge of the sac, the sac and door instantly open, drawing in water and the small creature. The door closes swiftly. Then, the bladderwort digests its victim for food.

16

As this first summer progresses, the spring peeper tadpoles eat and eat, and grow and grow. After about eight weeks, they are one inch long, and their tails are about half of that inch.

During this first summer, changes take place in the growing tadpoles. Almost miraculously, they prepare to leave behind their fishlike existence to take up life on land as tree frogs.

Gradually, buds of legs develop. Soon, their back legs break through to the outside and are visible. Webbing extends about halfway out between the back toes. Even the pads on their back toes can be seen. Now, their front legs appear.

At the same time, their lungs are developing and their gills are disappearing. Every once in a while, the tadpoles crawl part way out of the water on a grass stem, twig, or rock to use their new legs and try their developing lungs.

The characteristic crosslike markings begin to appear on their backs.

Soon their tails begin to shrink. The spring peeper tadpoles stop eating for part of this period of change. Their tails are gradually absorbed by their bodies as a source of nourishment. Eventually, the remainders of their tails disappear completely.

When they start eating again, the young spring peepers no longer seek algae or plant food. Now they catch flying insects, such as mosquitoes or gnats, with their long sticky tongues. A peeper's tongue is attached to the front of the bottom of its mouth (unlike ours which is attached at

the back of the bottom of our mouths). Because of the front attachment, it can whip out its tongue, capture a live insect on its sticky tip, and pull it back into its mouth almost faster than anyone can see it.

When all of the changes are complete, a young spring peeper breathes with its lungs and also through its skin. Because its skin has many tiny blood vessels in it, as well as mucous glands which always keep it moist, oxygen can enter directly through its skin into its bloodstream.

Each young spring peeper is only about as big as a housefly, but looks like an adult peeper. Now it is ready for life on land.

Like other frogs, spring peepers lead a double life. They are *amphibians*, which means that they spend part of their lives on land and part in the water. As we have seen, they must return to the water to reproduce.

During the months of July and August, the young spring peepers leave the pond. They and other emerging froglets are a new food supply for many of the animals of the woods, such as the weasels, skunks, snakes, and raccoons.

As they hop onto shore another enemy may come after them. Herons eat frogs. They often spear the larger species of frogs with their powerful beaks. However, many spring peepers manage to jump to safe hiding places in the bushes. The herons may be too busy catching other froglets coming ashore to pursue them. So again, some of the spring peepers survive.

The young spring peepers' main interest on land is to find and catch live insects to eat. They hop distances that are over ten times their body length. They cling with

20

their toe pads when they land. Each one pursues its own food.

The low bushes of the woods surrounding the water are a new home for the young spring peepers. There may be a mixture of white pine, oak, and maple trees in the woods. But close to the ground are lower bushes such as blueberry, fragrant sweet fern, pine seedlings, and scrub oak. These are where the spring peepers live. *Hyla crucifer* does not venture very high up from the ground as does the common tree frog, *Hyla versicolor*, and some of the other tree frog relatives.

As a peeper gets bigger, it outgrows the outer layer of its skin and sheds it. Usually, a flap of it comes loose first. The peeper may pull at the loose flap and begin to peel off the old skin. It rubs its back and belly. It squirms and stretches—anything to loosen and get rid of the old skin. Then it begins to eat the old skin as it comes away. Usually, all of the old skin is eaten. Underneath is a bright clean new skin. The outer layer of skin will be shed often in its lifetime and each time there will be a clean new skin underneath.

As late fall approaches, the days grow shorter and the nights longer and cooler. The spring peepers find places to hibernate in the woods. They crawl under loosened patches of moss or an insulating carpet of fallen leaves. The peepers will stay here for at least all of December and January. Some of the peepers will be safe and survive, barely alive, until spring arrives.

During hibernation, the spring peepers' heartbeats and breathing slow down, and they do not eat at all. Because they are cold-blooded animals, their bodies become the same temperature as their surroundings. When it is below 40° F., the spring peepers can get enough oxygen for survival through their skins alone.

Because spring peepers are very sensitive to temperature changes and to humidity, they are aware of the earliest hint of the warmth of spring. They may emerge as early as February.

In the milder climates of the South, spring peepers do not hibernate. They can be heard calling even in the winter months. The eggs are laid between November and March in these areas.

It will be three or four years from the time spring peepers are eggs in the pond before they are ready to reproduce themselves. The seasons pass and some survive to become mature.

In early spring, the males return to the water. Climbing onto a perch on a leaf or a few blades of grass, they start to call.

*Pee-EEp, Pee-EEp, Pee-EEp!*

Again, the male and female spring peepers join together this spring to lay fertile eggs in the water. Once more, the life cycle of the spring peeper is about to begin.

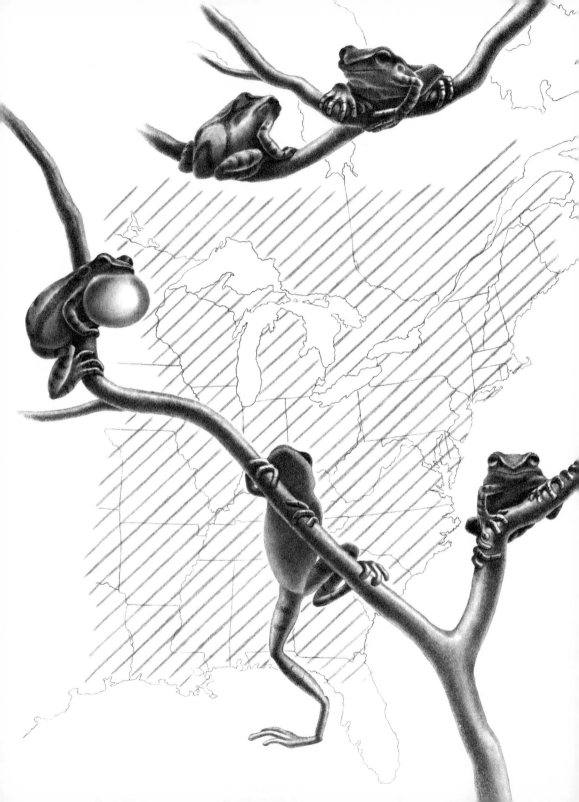

## Spring Peepers as Pets

Spring peepers, *Hyla crucifer*, are fascinating creatures to both young and adult nature lovers.

Spring peepers occupy a large range in both the United States and Canada. They are found throughout the states east of the Mississippi River, but only in the northern part of Florida. They are found as far west as eastern Oklahoma, Texas in the south, and central Minnesota and Iowa in the north. Peepers also can be found in Canada in southeastern Manitoba, across Ontario, in Quebec, and in the Maritime Provinces, except for Newfoundland. The large range affords many youngsters a chance to seek the elusive peeper.

Peepers are one of the earliest frogs to reproduce in the spring. Usually, in climates where hibernation occurs, all of the eggs have been laid by late May or mid-June.

25

Before you can collect spring peepers, you must find them. They are very difficult to see or catch. The best way to see a spring peeper is to search during the season when they are calling. Go at night with a flashlight and a friend. You can catch peepers with your hands if you are fast. A long-handled, fine-mesh, dip net is very helpful to reach peepers you may see in the water. You also need a container in which to carry them home. A coffee can with a snap-on plastic lid or a clear plastic jar is a good choice. The lid should have air holes punched in it. A handful of moist leaves or moss makes the container more comfortable for the peepers you catch.

As you approach an area where there is peeping, you must be very quiet. If the peepers stop singing, they are aware of you. Stand still and be quiet for a few minutes and they will start peeping again.

You must try to locate one voice and beam your light in that direction. You may be able to see the peeper's vibrating bubblelike vocal sac.

You will be amazed at how small and delicate these little frogs are. One reason not many people actually have seen a spring peeper is because they are so small and inconspicuous. After the eggs are laid, the adults leave the water and return to the woodlands. They are even harder to find in the woods than when they are near the water.

You will have to provide an aquarium or a large glass-sided container. You should furnish it with a wet area. Use a shallow dish of pond water, and fill in the bottom of the aquarium with sand up to the level of the edge of the dish. Now cover some of the sand with a layer of loamlike soil. You may want to place a few rocks and some patches of moss here and there to make it a more natural home for the peepers. Provide a few twigs or

small branches for them to climb. They will also cling to and climb on the glass of the container! Sometimes the peepers will swing like acrobats if you provide a miniature trapeze for them. It can be made out of a small stick and two pieces of string and hung from the twigs in the aquarium. Cover your aquarium with a piece of screening and weight it down with two or three boards so that your spring peepers cannot escape. Remember, they are excellent climbers and can fit through very small openings.

Spring peepers will eat live small insects, small worms, and small caterpillars. If you wish, you can keep a supply of mealworms in an old coffee can filled with moist bran. Mealworms can be obtained at most pet stores. If you dangle an insect or other suitable food in front of your peepers on a string, you will have a chance to see how they use their tongues to catch food.

You will find these little peepers delightful pets and can have fun watching them climb on the twigs and glass of the aquarium. They may even sing for you!

If you have a male and a female, maybe your spring peepers will produce some fertile eggs. Watch for them carefully, because the eggs are very tiny (1/12 of an inch). They look like small seeds.

You can also seek spring peeper eggs or tadpoles in low wetland areas where the eggs are laid in puddles or shallow pools of water. If you have heard the adults calling in such an area, you can be sure there are eggs being laid there. Look on the underwater stems of grasses and on fallen leaves from the bottoms of the pools. Scoop up debris from the bottoms of these pools and let it settle out. You may be delighted to see little tadpoles swimming about before your eyes. Now you can watch them change into adults.

You can also keep any tadpoles you find or that hatch in a small goldfish bowl or even a clean glass jar. They should be provided with pond water that has algae in it for food. Allow the algae to grow on the sides of the glass. You will see the tadpoles scraping it from the glass. If you must use any tap water, let it stand open for at least twenty-four hours to get rid of any chlorine in it. Do not place the bowl in direct sunlight. The water may become too warm and the tadpoles will die.

Provide a rock that sticks out of the water and that has a rather flat surface for the young tadpoles to rest on when their legs begin to appear. They will be starting to try their developing lungs then also.

You may release your extra frogs back at the pond site if you don't want to keep them.

Spring peepers have lived for several years in captivity. Of course, their lifespan in the wild is limited by chance encounters with their enemies.

Once you get acquainted with spring peepers, you will love their spring sound even more.

*Pee-EEp! Pee-EEp! Pee-EEp!*

## About the Author

CHARLENE W. BILLINGS was graduated from the University of New Hampshire, cum laude, with a degree in biology and Rivier College with a Master of Science degree. She has been a research assistant and has taught high school biology and junior high school science and mathematics.

Her long interest in science and her desire to impart some of the wonders of nature to children have led to this book on spring peepers.

Mrs. Billings lives in New Hampshire with her husband and two children.


## About the Illustrator

SUSAN BONNERS has illustrated several natural science books for children and has recently written and illustrated a book on the giant panda.

She attended the New York-Phoenix School of Design. Miss Bonners, a native of Chicago, presently lives in Brooklyn.